NADIYA'S

Bake Me
a Story
Festive

NADIYA'S

Bake Me a Story Festive

Nadiya Hussain

illustrated by Clair Rossiter

HODDER CHILDREN'S BOOKS

First published in Great Britain in 2017 by Hodder and Stoughton

1 3 5 7 9 10 8 6 4 2

Text copyright © Nadiya Hussain, 2017
Illustrations copyright © Clair Rossiter, 2017

Bake Me A Story is a registered trademark owned by Hodder & Stoughton Limited

The moral rights of the author and illustrator have been asserted.

A CIP catalogue record for this book
is available from the British Library.

ISBN 978 1 444 93961 3

Edited by Emma Goldhawk
Designed by Alison Padley

Photography by Adam Lawrence
Food photography by Georgia Glynn Smith
Food styling by Lisa Harrison

Printed and bound in Europe
by Mohn Media Mohndruck GmbH

The paper and board used in this book
are made from wood from responsible sources

MIX
Paper from
responsible sources
FSC® C104740

Hodder Children's Books
An imprint of
Hachette Children's Group
Part of Hodder and Stoughton
Carmelite House
50 Victoria Embankment
London EC4Y 0DZ

An Hachette UK Company
www.hachette.co.uk

www.hachettechildrens.co.uk

I never really understood what festivity was, until a
certain little boy came along in 1995. He showed me
that festivity is about celebrating, about imagination,
about love, about being with the people you love.
I learned that it is about the sparkle in the eyes of
the littlest people with the biggest hearts.

This book is for you, the little people in my life:
Shak, Musa, Dawud and Maryam.

Hi guys!

Fancy finding you here ... I'm Nadiya, and these are my three lovely kiddies, Musa, Dawud and Maryam. You may remember us from my first book, *Bake Me a Story*.

This book is a celebration of the two things that I love to do with my children the most — baking and sharing stories. And this time, everything has a festive twist to help you get ready for the best season of the year!

Inside you will find brand-new recipes, stories and poems perfect for the festive season. You could read the story or poem first and then make the recipes, or you could enjoy reading while your bakes are in the oven.

Maybe you'd like to read my poem about The Little Fir Tree while your Christmas ginger cake bakes, or enjoy the story of The Nutcracker and then make your own nut roast. Or, you might like to meet the Snow Queen and eat her doughnut bread pudding, or discover where your odd socks go while you munch on some cheesy feet biscuits!

The festive season can mean so many different things to all of us. For me and my family, it's a time to have fun and be excited, but it's also a time for kindness and caring. It's a time to be with the people you love.

I always love to see my readers' bakes, so don't forget to use #BakeMeAStory when you post pictures on social media!

So, stick some holly in your hair, whack on your apron and get into the kitchen with us – it's time to get busy as we bake and share more stories.

Happy holidays!

Love, Nadiya

Musa

Dawud

Maryam

xxxx

HELPFUL HINTS AND TASTY TIPS

Safety in the kitchen

Always make sure a grown-up is with you in the kitchen.

Don't touch the kitchen knives – they are sharp! If a grown-up says you can use them to chop or slice, be very careful.

Ask a grown-up to help you if you are using a food processor.

Always wash your hands in warm soapy water before you start.

Be careful of the hot oven and hobs.

Oven temperature

All the recipes in this book have been tested in a fan-assisted oven. If you are using a conventional oven, increase the temperature by 20°C.

Measurements

g – grams
ml – millilitres
tsp – teaspoon
tbsp – tablespoon
°C – degrees celsius

Recipe guide

Every recipe has a guide to show you how easy or difficult it might be. Always make sure a grown-up is with you when you try any of these recipes, especially when it needs a knife or a food processor, or involves anything hot.

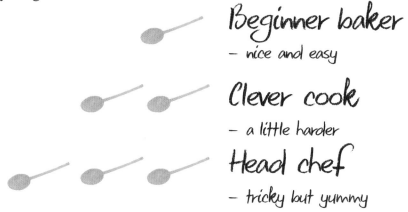

Beginner baker
– nice and easy

Clever cook
– a little harder

Head chef
– tricky but yummy

CONTENTS

Where the Other
SOCKS GO

Have you ever hung out your wet laundry
And wondered where one sock has gone?
You know there were two to begin with
When you switched the washing machine on.

You see, there's a very big secret
That all of your socks surely know,
They keep it hush-hush from their owners:
That place where the other socks go.

Your socks in the drawer have a purpose
Nestled snugly, paired up with their twin,
Waiting for you to select them
And your warm-footed day to begin.

2

The socks do their job in the day time
On your cheeeesy feet they must stay,
Then they patiently wait in the basket,
'Til it's finally washing machine day.

Then into the drum they get loaded
Round and round, in the soapiest suds,
They get rather dizzy from rolling
And trying to swim through the flood.

They know that it's waiting there for them,
Through the drum and the bubbly swirls,
It's the land where the other socks head for:
The Sock Land of Glitter and Pearls.

A place where no odd sock is ordinary
Each one with its very own style,
Covered with glitter and sparkles,
They wish they could stay for a while.

But now that they have a new purpose
They have to come back from that place
What do you think that they do now?
It will put a wide smile on your face …

Those stockings you hang up at Christmas
They might not come straight from a store.
They've been to the Sock Land of Glitter
And returned as so very much more.

Remember this magical secret
When you're searching for one missing sock,
They've gone to that big Land of Glitter
To come back as stockings that ROCK!

CHEESY FEET BISCUITS

The kids and I love making biscuits together, but we tend to stick to sweet biscuits. Savoury biscuits are just as tasty and just as fun - especially if you decide to decorate them before you tuck in! The recipe for the Red Pepper Dip you can use as a base for the decorations is on the next page.

Makes 12

Ingredients

200g unsalted butter, cold and cubed

200g plain flour, sifted, (plus extra for
the work surface)

200g mature Cheddar cheese,
finely grated

1 tsp mustard powder

1 tsp garlic granules

5 tbsp water

Pop some baking paper over the top of this template and trace your own stocking shape.

Method

- In a medium bowl, rub the butter into the flour with your fingertips until the mixture resembles breadcrumbs.

- Add the cheese, mustard powder and garlic granules. Add the water – you may not need all of it if your dough is very sticky and you can always add a touch more if it's dry. Then, bring the dough together into a mound.

- Wrap the dough in cling film and chill for 30 minutes in the fridge.

- Line two baking trays with baking paper. Take more baking paper and trace over the template of the stocking. Ask a grown-up to help you cut it out.

- Dust the work surface with flour and roll the chilled dough out until it is about 0.5cm thick.

- Lay your template on the dough and ask a grown-up to help you cut around it with a knife. Take each stocking and put them on the prepared baking trays.

- Chill the biscuits in the fridge for 20 minutes, or until firm to the touch.

- Preheat the oven to 170°C fan/gas mark 5.

- When they are firm, prick the base of all the biscuits with a fork. This will let air escape, making them nice and flat for decorating later.

- Bake for 20 minutes, then remove from the oven and leave to cool on the tray for 15 minutes.

- Transfer the biscuits to a wire rack and leave to cool completely.

Now turn over to make the Red Pepper Dip and decorate your biscuits!

7

RED PEPPER DIP

This roasted red pepper dip is a great base to help your decorations stick to the biscuits, and it tastes great too! You can be as creative with your cheesy feet toppings as you like. I've used grated Cheddar cheese, pitted and sliced olives and chives.

Ingredients

1 tbsp olive oil

1 small red onion, chopped

1 garlic clove, peeled and crushed

1 anchovy fillet, chopped

150g roasted red peppers from a jar, drained and roughly chopped

To decorate:

70g mature Cheddar cheese, grated

30g green olives, sliced

30g black olives, sliced

10g chives, chopped

Method

- Put the oil and onion in a small non-stick saucepan on a medium heat and cook for 3 minutes.
- Add the garlic and anchovy and cook for a further 2 minutes, until the onions are soft.
- Add the peppers and cook for 5 minutes, until all the moisture has evaporated.
- Place the mixture in a blender and whizz until very smooth.
- Transfer to a bowl and leave to cool.
- To decorate your biscuits, spread them with the cooled red pepper dip and add your toppings!

NADIYA'S TIP
Store the leftover anchovies in an airtight container in the fridge so you can use them in other dishes. I sometimes add them to a tomato sauce, or pop them on pizzas.

The
SNOW QUEEN

Many many moons ago, in the icy village of Arderdale, there lived an evil troll. He had a magic mirror which helped him spy on all the villagers and do evil things to them. Eventually, the villagers got so fed up of the troll's evil deeds, they banished him to live far beyond the earth, in the furthest reaches of the sky.

Kye and Gaby were best friends. They'd known each other since they were tiny, and they would climb in and out of each other's houses to spend time together. Both Kye and Gaby loved Arderdale, but they didn't really like the cold, and would spend hours telling each other tales of the hot places they would visit together when they grew up. The only good thing about living somewhere that was always freezing was the ice cream.

One day, Gaby climbed through Kye's window. Kye had invited her over because his Gran had made her doughnut bread pudding, and they could warm up with a bowl of it while listening to Gran's stories around the fire. Gran served up three bowls of the steaming, custardy pudding and started to tell the story of The Snow Queen. It was one Kye and Gaby hadn't heard before. They cuddled up under a blanket, their arms wrapped around each other like best friends do.

"There is a lady who once lived amongst us," Gran began, "a lady who always wore a fur coat. They say a shard of ice lodged in her heart and made her into a cruel Snow Queen. Now she comes back to the village to put people under a spell with just a touch, then she leads them back to her palace at the edge of the woods with a promise of never-ending ice cream. And you know how much Arderdale loves ice cream! Only, when the people get back to the palace she makes them her slaves, to polish her ice palace and keep it cold. There's never any ice cream."

Suddenly, a huge gust of wind blew under the gap in the front door and hit Kye full in the face. Little did they know that on the wind was something evil indeed. Up beyond the clouds, the troll had accidentally dropped his magic mirror and it had tumbled out of the sky, smashing into pieces on the ground below. As the wind blew into Arderdale, tiny splinters of magic mirror-glass were carried with it, and they were flying into the villagers' eyes. The splinters were turning even the kindest villagers into mean, unkind people.

Kye suddenly pulled the blanket over him, leaving Gaby shivering. Then he pinched her on the arm, hard. "Go away, Gaby," Kye said.

"I don't want to share my pudding or my gran's stories with you any more."

Gaby burst into tears and ran home, an angry red mark already rising on her arm.

The next day, as Kye walked to school with an angry scowl on his face, he bumped into a lady in a fur coat. He looked up at her, ready to say something rude, but as soon as he looked into her ice-blue eyes, he found he couldn't move his tongue. She touched him lightly on the arm, and he found himself following her into the icy woods.

The villagers looked for Kye for days and days. Nobody knew where he had disappeared to. Gaby knew deep down that something had happened to her friend. Even though he had been really mean to her, Gaby still loved Kye and missed him terribly, so she went to his gran for help.

"What can break the Snow Queen's spell?" she begged.

"Only the warm hug of a true friend and something warm for their tummy," Gran replied. "It's a good job I've been baking today ..."

So after a short while, Gaby set off into the woods with a huge tub of Gran's doughnut pudding in her rucksack.

After a terrifying hike to the edge of Arderdale, Gaby found the Snow Queen's palace.

Peering through the icy windows, she could see lots of villagers, and among them, Kye. He was kneeling on the floor, blue and shivering from cold. Gaby's heart broke for her friend and she cried, her tears running down the icy window and melting a hole just big enough for Gaby to climb through. She slipped and slid her way over the icy floor to her best friend and grabbed him in the biggest, warmest hug she could. He felt like he'd not had a good meal in a long time, and he shook with cold.

Gaby's tears fell on Kye's face and washed the mirror splinter from his eye. He looked up at her like he'd not seen anything clearly for a very long time.

"Kye! I thought we'd lost you forever," Gaby wept. "Quick, your gran gave me this. Eat it, warm yourself up." Kye ate a bite of the warm doughnut pudding and felt better straightaway.

The rest of the villagers began to cry at the happy sight of Kye and Gaby hugging, and their falling tears began to melt the ice palace. The Snow Queen was furious, but before she could do anything, Kye thrust the rest of the pudding at her. She couldn't resist its smell and ate a huge spoonful. As if by magic, the warmth of the pudding melted the shard of ice in the Snow Queen's heart and she cried too, harder than all of the captive villagers put together.

"I am so sorry for treating you all so cruelly," she said. "I don't know what came over me. Now my ice palace is melted,

I will become a villager again, as I was so many years ago. And I am sorry I promised you all never-ending ice cream and never gave you any."

"That's all right," Gaby said. "We can all go back to Arderdale together and be happy again."

"And my gran makes the best ice cream in the world, so we'll stop off there on the way home," said Kye.

Then Kye took one of the Snow Queen's hands and Gaby took the other and led everyone back to the village they all loved.

TREACLE SEMIFREDDO

The combination of sweet and smoky flavours in this ice cream is really amazing. Best of all, you don't need to churn it in a machine – you just leave it to set in the freezer and it'll be perfect. Brrrr!

Serves 8-10

Ingredients

1 large egg

4 large egg yolks

100g treacle, plus extra for drizzling

300ml double cream

Method

❄ Line a 900g loaf tin with cling film, making sure that you have plenty of overhang. You'll use that later to cover the base of the semifreddo.

❄ Put the whole egg, egg yolks and treacle in a heatproof bowl that can fit comfortably on the top of a saucepan.

❄ Put a few inches of water in the bottom of the pan and heat to a simmer.

❄ Place the heatproof bowl on top of the pan, making sure that it doesn't touch the water. Whisk the mixture until light and fluffy, and paler in colour. This will take a few minutes.

❄ Take off the heat, set aside and allow to cool.

❄ Whip the cream in a separate bowl until it forms stiff peaks.

❄ Add the egg mixture to the cream and fold through to combine.

❄ Pour the mixture into the lined tin. Use the overhanging cling film to cover the top of the tin (the base of the semifreddo).

❄ Leave to set in the freezer for at least 6 hours, or overnight if possible.

❄ Once frozen, unwrap the tin and lift the ice cream out onto a platter or flat plate. Remove the cling film and drizzle with treacle.

❄ Slice and serve immediately.

DOUGHNUT BREAD AND BUTTER PUDDING

This is the perfect treat to curl up with on cold winter days. It's warm and custardy and oh-so comforting – especially if the weather is bad outside. A little bowl of this rich pudding will go a long way!

Serves 9

Ingredients

butter, for greasing

6 jam doughnuts

200ml whole milk

300ml double cream

1 tsp vanilla extract or vanilla bean paste

40g caster sugar

3 large eggs

1 tsp icing sugar

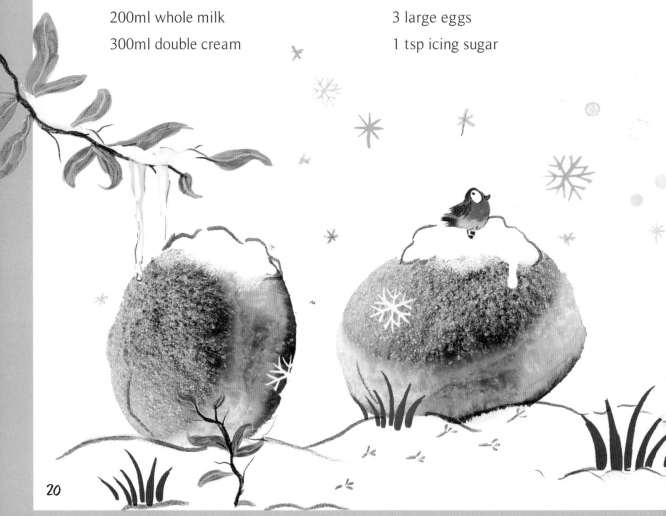

Method

❄ Generously grease a 23cm square ovenproof dish.

❄ Cut the doughnuts in half horizontally to make two circles. Lay these in the dish with the jam facing up.

❄ Whisk the milk, cream, vanilla, sugar and eggs together in a jug until well combined.

❄ Pour the mixture over the doughnuts, gently pressing them down so they are submerged.

❄ Put the dish to one side for 30 minutes, so the doughnuts can soak up the mixture.

❄ Preheat the oven to 170°C fan/gas mark 5.

❄ Bake in the oven for 30–35 minutes, until the custardy centre of the pudding is slightly wobbly.

❄ Set aside to cool for 10 minutes. Dust with the icing sugar before serving.

The Little
TEALIGHT GIRL

Eight-year-old Mabel was a quiet, thoughtful girl. The two things Mabel loved the most in the whole wide world were doing colouring-in, and her Nanna. It was the best feeling in the world when she got to do colouring-in *with* her Nanna. But Nanna had died last Christmas, and Mabel had felt too sad to do colouring-in since.

Now it was December the 24th and Mabel was sitting in her dad's café. Mabel didn't drink coffee – she thought it tasted bitter and smelled funny. But she had to go somewhere in the school holidays, especially now Nanna wasn't there to look after her when Dad was at work.

Mabel wasn't looking forward to Christmas. It would be the first Christmas without Nanna, and she knew she and Dad were going to miss her so much. She thought about the pancakes Nanna always insisted on serving for breakfast on Christmas morning. She thought about the truffles that Dad always made for Nanna and she always ate after Christmas dinner, even though she said she was about to go pop. Those things wouldn't happen ever again. Mabel poked at the glass of eggnog in front of her and sighed.

"How are you doing, Mabel?" Jess, the waitress in the café asked. "I thought you looked a bit sad, so I popped out and got you something to cheer you up."

Jess pushed a carrier bag across the table. Mabel opened the bag and pulled out a pack of pencils in all colours of the rainbow, and … a colouring-in book. Mabel didn't have the heart to tell Jess about why this present made her feel sadder, so she smiled and said her best thank you. Mabel was also a brave little girl.

It was getting dark outside, so Jess got busy lighting the tealights on the café's tables. Mabel's eyes followed the little orange flames as each one sparked and flickered. Her eyelids started to feel heavy … sooooo heavy …

"Mabel, sweetheart."

Mabel blinked. It couldn't be. That was Nanna's voice! She blinked again, hard. There Nanna was, sat across the table beaming at her granddaughter, her hands wrapped around the glass of eggnog.

"I always loved this stuff," Nanna said with a wink.

Mabel reached out for her. "I miss you so much," she said. "I can't celebrate Christmas without you."

"Of course you can," said Nanna. "Go to the cupboard beside the cooker when you get home. My recipe book is in there. You and your dad can make it the best Christmas you ever had. I love you, Mabel."

Mabel blinked again, and Nanna was gone.

Somehow, Mabel didn't feel sad any more. When she and Dad got home, she went straight to the cupboard and pulled out the recipe book. Mabel and her dad cooked all their usual Christmas treats together, and Dad told Mabel lots of funny stories about Nanna. Before Mabel went to bed, she even did some colouring-in. It was definitely the best Christmas Eve ever.

And from that day on, every time she missed Nanna, Mabel would sit in the warm glow of a tealight, close her eyes and picture Dad's funny stories in her head. It would always make her smile.

TURKEY AND SPINACH PANCAKES

Pancakes are brilliant at breakfast, lovely at lunch and delicious at dinner! These pancakes have a turkey filling, in honour of the traditional Christmas dinner, but you could fill them with anything you fancy. You can eat them at any time of day you fancy, too!

Makes 12

Ingredients

110g plain flour, sifted

salt and pepper

280ml whole milk

2 large eggs

spray oil for frying

400g mature Cheddar cheese, finely grated

4 large handfuls of baby spinach

320g turkey ham, thinly sliced

Method

- Put the flour in a bowl, season with salt and pepper, and mix well.

- Measure out the milk in a measuring jug, then add the eggs and whisk.

- Make a well in the centre of the flour and pour in the egg mixture. Whisk until you have no lumps in the batter.

- Place a 20cm non-stick frying pan on a medium to high heat.

- Spray the pan with oil and add 2 tablespoons of the batter. Swirl the batter around the pan to create a thin, even layer.

- Cook for 30 seconds, then use a palette knife to flip the pancake over to cook on the other side.

- Scatter with cheese and spinach and lay some turkey on top. Fold the pancake in half and cook folded for 1 minute or until the cheese has just melted.

- Place on a plate and cover with foil while you cook the rest of the pancakes.

CHOCOLATE ORANGE EGG NOG

Eggnog is a traditional Christmas drink, and my version adds a delicious twist. It's like drinking a chocolate bar in a cup! The recipe does contain raw eggs though, so it shouldn't be served to babies and toddlers, pregnant women, or elderly people.

Makes 8-10 small glasses

Ingredients

6 large eggs

20g cocoa powder, sifted, plus extra for dusting

170g tin of condensed milk

1 tsp vanilla

1 litre skimmed milk

grated zest of 1 orange

150ml double cream

ice cubes, to serve

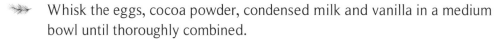

Method

➤ Whisk the eggs, cocoa powder, condensed milk and vanilla in a medium bowl until thoroughly combined.

➤ Add the milk and orange zest and mix well.

➤ In a separate bowl, whip the cream to soft peaks.

➤ Add the whipped cream to the egg mixture and whisk again to combine.

➤ Pour into a jug and leave to chill in the fridge until you're ready to serve.

➤ Serve in small glasses with ice cubes, dusted with a little cocoa powder.

31

SPECULOOS COCONUT TRUFFLES

These bite-sized truffles are some of the easiest treats you and your children can make together. They look so pretty when they're finished, you could even pop some in a gift box and give them to friends and family as presents.

Makes 30-35

Ingredients

250g speculoos biscuits (lotus biscuits)

397g tin of condensed milk

220g desiccated coconut

You will also need

30–35 mini cupcake cases

Method

↠ Place the biscuits into a large zip-lock food bag. Using a rolling pin, crush the biscuits to a fine crumb.

↠ Pour the crushed biscuits into a bowl, then add the condensed milk and 120g of the desiccated coconut and mix together well.

↠ Pour the rest of the coconut into a shallow dish.

↠ Using clean hands, take a walnut-sized amount of the biscuit mixture and roll into small balls.

↠ Roll each ball in the coconut and place in a mini cupcake case.

Who is the Lady in the
RED MERCEDES?

Hannah, Henry, Harriet and Harper were squished on the sofa. It was Christmas Eve, and they were completely knackered after following Mum around the packed supermarket for a whole afternoon. Being a kid at Christmas was such a tough business …

"Did you see that guy shove other guy who'd grabbed the last bag of Brussels sprouts?" Harriet said to Harper.

"I know!" Harper said. "And no one eats sprouts anyway."

"Er – I do!" Henry piped up. "And they taste even better the next day in Mum's Bubble and Squeak."

Hannah didn't say anything. She was too busy filling her mouth with huge forkfuls of the orange frangipane tart they always had on Christmas Eve. It was a special recipe Mum baked every year that was handed down from their grandpa.

Harper, Harriet and Henry grabbed themselves a slice each, knowing they couldn't leave it too long or Hannah would scoff the lot.

Then Henry stopped suddenly, his fork halfway to his mouth. "Bells!" he gasped.

There was a faint CHING CHING CHING sound, coming from outside. That could only mean one thing.

All four kids dashed to the window and peered through the shutters. But there was no sign of Santa, just a lady climbing out of a tomato-red Mercedes. She was dressed from head to toe in red, apart from her white furry hat.

As the lady walked to the boot of her car, there was the CHING CHING CHING sound again. The kids squinted up at the sky, but there was still no sign of a sleigh, or—

"Reindeer!" Harper squealed. "Look! A reindeer! There, on the back seat!"

There was a flash of antlers as a reindeer lifted its head to sniff the air. But it disappeared from sight so quickly, the kids weren't sure if they had imagined it.

The lady shut the boot and slung a big bulky bag across her back.

The kids stared at each other.

"Are you thinking what I'm thinking?" Hannah said.

"Yep," Harriet agreed. "But Santa's a man, not a lady ... Isn't he?"

They peeked through the shutters, watching as the lady in red walked up and down their street, stopping at each of their neighbours' doors. Her big sack seemed to get emptier each time she stopped, but under the dim streetlights, they couldn't quite see what she was doing. She got closer, and closer, and closer... then, she walked up to their front door!

All four kids immediately ducked down from the window. Everyone knew that if you saw Santa, you wouldn't get presents.

And even though the lady *definitely* wasn't Santa, they thought they'd better not risk it.

"Could I just leave this parcel with you?" They heard the lady say, once Mum had answered the door. "It's for your neighbour, but they don't seem to be home."

"Would you like to come in, Mrs C?" Mum said. She loved having visitors. "You look tired, and I have a slice of my orange frangipane tart going spare ..."

"That's so kind," the lady replied, "but I'm afraid I can't. I found an injured reindeer by the side of the road, and I need to get him to the vet before they close for Christmas. Better dash." And off she went, the CHING CHING CHING loud and clear now.

Hannah, Henry, Harriet and Harper peered out from behind the sofa, where they had hidden to listen to the lady and mum chatting.

"What on earth are you doing behind there?" Mum said, poking her head into the living room. "Right, you lot! Upstairs, brush your teeth. You know it's early bedtime on Christmas Eve!"

The kids huddled around the sink and wiggled their eyebrows at each other while they brushed their teeth. Suddenly, DING DONG – someone else was at the door.

They hurried to spit out their toothpaste foam so they could get downstairs and see who the new visitor was, but they were too late. By the time they got down there, Mum had already said goodbye.

"Who was it, who was it, who was it?" they all shouted over each other.

"The lady from earlier," Mum said with a grin. "She realised she had forgotten to do something ..."

And with that, Mum pushed open the door to the living room. There was a pile of brightly coloured presents, sitting beneath the Christmas tree.

"Who is she, Mummy?" Henry gasped.

"That's Mrs C, darling, but everyone knows her as Mary. She's from the Special North Pole Delivery Service. Only get to see her once a year."

A timer went off, and mum headed back to the kitchen. The kids rushed to the shutters and peeked through them again.

Mary C was stood outside. She tucked her hair behind her ears, revealing big jangly earrings made from bells. Then, she looked up and gave the kids a wave and a wink, before getting into her red Mercedes and driving away.

CARDAMOM AND MARMALADE FRANGIPANE TART

Just like in the story, this tart won't last long once it's served up! There's lots in the method that kids of every age can manage: younger children could do the sifting, while older children could be in charge of making the 'breadcrumbs' or spreading the marmalade.

Makes 6

Ingredients

For the pastry

150g unsalted butter, cold and cubed

225g plain flour, plus extra for the work surface

25g icing sugar

1 large egg, beaten

2 tbsp cold water

For the filling

grated zest of 1 orange

4 tbsp fine shred marmalade

150g unsalted butter, softened

150g caster sugar

150g ground almonds

1 tsp ground cardamom powder

1 large egg, beaten

For the icing

250g icing sugar

3 tbsp orange juice

grated zest of 1 orange

Method

- In a medium bowl, rub the butter into the flour with your fingertips until the mixture resembles breadcrumbs.

- Sieve the icing sugar into the 'breadcrumbs' and mix through.

- Make a well in centre of the mixture and add the beaten egg and water. Mix it all together with a palette knife, then bring the dough together with your hands.

- Wrap the pastry in cling film and chill for 30 minutes in the fridge.

- Dust the work surface with flour and roll the chilled pastry out until it is as thin as possible – ideally about 2mm.

- Gently lift the pastry into a 20cm tart tin. Push it into the corners and leave 2cm hanging over the edge.

- Place on a baking tray and chill for a further 15 minutes.

- Preheat the oven to 180°C fan/gas mark 6.

- Line the inside of the tin with baking paper, on top of the chilled pastry, then pour some baking beans onto the paper. If you don't have baking beans, you could use dried lentils, or rice, or any other dried pulses.

- Bake for 15 minutes, then take it out of the oven. Remove the beads and paper.

- Put the pastry back in the oven for another 5 minutes, then remove and let it cool a little. Trim the edge of the pastry so it sits flush with the top of the tin.

- Lower the oven temperature to 160°C fan/gas mark 4.

- Mix the orange zest into the marmalade, then spread the marmalade in an even layer over the bottom of the pastry case.

- Cream the butter and sugar in a medium bowl until light and fluffy.

- Add the almonds and cardamom and mix together.

- Thoroughly stir in the beaten egg, spoon the mixture on top of the marmalade and spread evenly.

- Bake the tart for 30 minutes, then remove from the oven and leave to cool in the tin for at least 30 minutes.

- To make the icing, mix the icing sugar and orange juice in a bowl until you have a smooth paste.

- Pour the icing over the top of the cooled tart and sprinkle with the orange zest.

Friends With
NO DOORS

Tilly loved animals. She had a dog named Fluff, two cats, Fish and Chips, and a lizard called Dennis.

Tilly's house was always mad. There was homework, dog biscuits and cat fur everywhere. It was especially mad at Christmas, when tinsel, half-written Christmas cards and gingerbread crumbs were everywhere too.

Even though everything was mad, Tilly's family always did something special for the other people who lived on their road at Christmas. Every year, they would make a tasty gift of biscotti for every neighbour whose front door they could see from the window at the front of their house. They would wrap the biscotti in special paper and tie each package with brightly coloured ribbon. It was one of Tilly's favourite things to do at Christmas.

But this year was different. They were not making tasty gifts for their neighbours, they were saying goodbye to them. Tilly and her family were moving to a new house.

Everyone packed their boxes and Tilly packed her toys. Then she got Fluff, Fish and Chips, and Dennis comfortable in their carry cases. It was time to leave.

A long drive later, the family pulled up outside their new house. It was by a forest in the middle of the countryside, and there were no other houses around.

"I can't see any front doors from here," Tilly said in a quiet voice.

Dad gave Tilly a squeeze. "Don't worry, Till, you'll make new friends when you go to school."

As Tilly unpacked her toys she felt sad. She gazed out of the window at the nearby forest, wishing she was back at the old house, handing out biscotti to the neighbours. Even after a cuddle with Fluff and a chat with Dennis, she still felt sad.

Suddenly, there was a flurry of brown and a flash of red at the window. It was a robin, settling down on a nearby branch. Tilly gasped. She'd had a wonderful idea!

The next morning, Tilly and her family pulled on their wellies and headed out into the forest. Tilly was carrying a bulging bag.

They stopped beside an oak tree with low-hanging branches.

"I think this one will do nicely, don't you, Tilly?" Mum said.

Tilly reached into her bag and pulled out a knobbly ball that was attached to a piece of string. It was a bird feeder. Tilly and her parents had been up all night making them, just for today.

She stretched up to one of the branches and tied the bird feeder to the branch with a piece of the colourful ribbon she'd saved from last year's biscotti bags.

"Here you go, birdies." Tilly called. "We know finding food can be hard at this time of year, so this is a gift from us to you."

And even though they couldn't see front doors from their window any more, there were still neighbours Tilly and her family could give gifts to at Christmas.

NUTTY LIME BISCOTTI

In my house, as in Tilly's, it's a festive tradition to deliver a baked gift to all the neighbours whose front doors we can see from our doorstep. These biscotti make a great gift. You could wrap them up in baking paper and tie the parcel with bright ribbon, or pop them in a cellophane bag to make the gift extra special.

Makes 32

Ingredients

100g mixed nuts, roughly chopped

100g mixed peel

grated zest of 1 lime

275g plain flour, plus extra for
   the work surface

½ tsp baking powder

150g caster sugar

3 large eggs, lightly beaten

Method

Preheat the oven to 160°C fan/gas mark 4. Line a baking tray with baking paper.

Put the nuts, mixed peel, lime zest, flour, baking powder and sugar in a medium bowl. Give it a good stir, then dust the work surface with flour – you're about to get your hands messy!

Make a well in the centre of the mixture and pour in the beaten eggs.

Mix with a spatula at first, then when the dough is starting to form, bring it together with your hands.

Transfer the dough to the floured work surface and without kneading too much more, make a sausage shape roughly 30x5cm.

Lift the sausage gently on to the baking tray, then flatten it slightly with your hands.

Bake in the oven for 25 minutes.

Take it out and leave to cool on the tray for 30 minutes.

Turn the oven down to 130°C fan/gas mark 2.

Cut the biscotti into 1cm-thick slices. Remove the baking paper from the cooled tray, then lay the slices flat on the tray. You may need two trays now.

Bake for another 15 minutes, then turn the biscotti over and continue baking for a final 15 minutes until the biscotti are crisp and golden.

Take out of the oven and leave to cool on a wire rack.

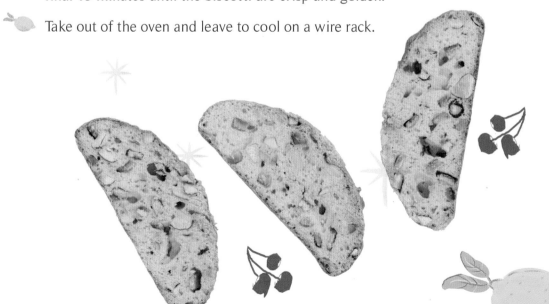

TILLY'S BIRD FEEDER

You might like to make a bird feeder like Tilly's. They're not for humans to eat though, so make them for your feathered friends only! You should only put these feeders out when it is cold, as the fat could melt in summer and coat the birds' wings.

You will need

200g lard or suet

400g of any of the following:

wild bird seed, currants, sultanas,

oats, bread or cake crumbs,

grated cheese, peanuts

For hanging

twine or string

Method

Place all your dry ingredients together in a bowl and mix.

Melt the lard or suet in a medium pan then add the dry mixture. Stir until the fat has been absorbed and the mixture sticks together.

Wait for the mix to cool slightly, then grab a handful and a length of string and squeeze the mixture around the string, shaping it into a ball. You could shape more than one ball around the string if you would like to.

Place the balls on a baking tray and put them in the fridge overnight to set.

Tie a big knot at the base of the string, as close to the bottom of the balls as possible, to secure them.

Hang them up from a branch and watch the birds enjoy their winter treat.

The Little
FIR TREE

There were some woods not far from us,
The trees were lush and green.
They were the biggest fir trees
That we had ever seen.

Towards the sky they grew and grew,
They almost touched the sun.
Their branches spreading far and wide
They shaded everyone.

Beneath these towering giants,
Grew one teeny tiny tree.
She really was a little 'un.
As small as small could be.

The bigger fir trees in the wood,
They used to laugh and jeer
At the teeny tiny fir tree,
Who longed to disappear.

"You'll never be as tall as us,
You'll never be as good."
So in their giant shadows
The Little Fir Tree stood.

One day a child came along
To choose a Christmas tree.
"Let's have this one, Mummy,
It's dinky, just like me!"

They took the Little Fir Tree home,
It wasn't very far.
Her branches fitted snugly
In the backseat of the car.

"Welcome home," the child said,
As they planted her in the ground.
"I can't wait to make you pretty,
Now Christmas has come around."

"But before the decorations,
We've a special thing to make.
It's tradition in our family –
The Christmas ginger cake!"

The Little Fir Tree watched the child
In the kitchen, having fun.
He sieved and stirred and licked the bowl
And iced biscuits, one by one.

Then while the cake was baking,
The child came outdoors.
"I've finished making my treat,
so now, it's time for yours ..."

Tinsel, bells and baubles,
And on top, a star of gold.
He made her shine and sparkle,
Out there in the cold.

The child stood back, admired his work
With pleasure in his eyes.
"You really are majestic,
No matter what your size."

The Little Fir Tree was so proud,
She felt extremely tall.
Her little boy thought she was
The most special tree of all.

She forgot the jeers and teasing
From the lofty trees above.
She was now a little Christmas tree,
Who'd found a home … and love.

CHRISTMAS GINGER CAKE

When I smell ginger, it makes me think of Christmas. Here are two recipes that are packed with ginger – you can make just the cake, or just the biscuits (recipe on the next page). Or, if you have time, you can put them all together to make one gingery wowzer of a Christmas cake!

Serves 12

Ingredients

For the cake

375ml whole milk

165g soft light brown sugar

1 tsp bicarbonate of soda

150g unsalted butter

250g golden syrup

300g self-raising flour, sifted

2 tbsp ground ginger

1 tbsp ground cinnamon

65g stem ginger, finely grated
   (plus 80ml of syrup from the jar)

1 large egg, beaten

For the buttercream icing (if you are making the cake and the biscuits, double these quantities for a big batch of icing)

75g unsalted butter, softened

150g icing sugar, sifted

2½ tbsp whole milk

pinch of ground cinnamon

Method

- Preheat the oven to 160°C fan/gas mark 4. Grease and line the base and sides of a 25cm round cake tin and line with baking paper. Don't use a loose-bottomed tin, as the cake mixture will be quite liquid.

- Heat the milk and sugar in a medium pan over a low heat. Just before it comes to the boil, take it off the heat. Add the bicarbonate of soda and stir through. Set aside until it is cool to the touch.

- Heat the butter and syrup in a small pan over a low heat until the butter has melted. Set aside to cool slightly.

- Mix the flour, ground ginger and cinnamon in a bowl to combine. Add the cooled milk mixture, the butter mixture, the stem ginger and syrup, and the beaten egg.

- Give it a good stir with a whisk, until all the lumps have gone.

- Pour into the prepared tin and bake for 55 minutes to 1 hour on the middle shelf until the cake is slightly coming away from the edge of the tin. Check the cake is baked by inserting a skewer into the middle. If the skewer comes out clean, the cake's ready.

- Remove from the oven and leave in the tin for 15 minutes to cool slightly. Then remove from the tin, transfer to a wire rack and leave to cool completely.

- Make the buttercream icing by putting the butter, icing sugar, milk and cinnamon in a bowl. Whisk with an electric mixer until light and fluffy.

- Once the cake has cooled, spread half of the icing on top of the cake with a spatula. Remember to use only half if you made a double quantity – you'll need the other half to ice the biscuits if you are making these too.

LITTLE FIR TREE BISCUITS

These ginger biscuits are crisp on the outside and chewy on the inside – Christmas never tasted so good! Will you cover your tree in baubles or will it look like it has come straight from the forest? It doesn't matter, as long as you enjoy decorating it.

Makes 1 large biscuit plus 24 small biscuits

Ingredients

2 tbsp golden syrup

1 large egg yolk

200g self-raising flour, plus extra for
   the work surface

½ tsp bicarbonate of soda

1 tsp ground ginger

2 tsp ground cinnamon

100g unsalted butter, cold and cubed

75g soft light brown sugar

For the buttercream icing (if you are
making the biscuits and the cake, double
these quantities for a big batch of icing)

75g unsalted butter, softened

150g icing sugar, sifted

2 ½ tbsp whole milk

pinch of ground cinnamon

For the decorations

70g desiccated coconut

¼ tsp green gel food colouring

coloured dragees for decorations

1 yellow fondant star for the top of
   the large tree

You will also need

1 x 12cm tree cutter and 1 x 6cm tree
cutter

Method

- Preheat the oven to 160°C fan/gas mark 4. Line two baking trays with baking paper.

- Mix the syrup and egg yolk together in a small bowl, then set aside.

- In a medium bowl, mix the flour, bicarbonate of soda, ginger and cinnamon until combined.

- Add the butter and, using your fingertips, rub it into the flour mixture until it resembles breadcrumbs.

- Add the sugar to the 'breadcrumbs' and stir through. Now add the syrup/egg mixture and, using your hands, bring the dough together.

- Dust the work surface and your rolling pin with flour. Roll out the dough until it is about 3mm thick.

- Using the large cutter, cut out one tree and place it on one of the trays. Using the small cutter, cut out 24 trees and place on the trays.

- Chill the trays in the fridge for 20 minutes so the biscuits will firm up and keep their shape while baking.

- After chilling, bake the biscuits for 12 minutes.

- Remove from the oven and leave to cool on the tray for 20 minutes, then transfer to a wire rack to cool completely.

For the icing and decoration

- Make the buttercream icing by putting the butter, icing sugar, milk and cinnamon in a bowl. Whisk with an electric mixer until light and fluffy.

- Put the desiccated coconut and the food colouring into a zip-lock food bag, seal and mix by shaking the bag or mushing its contents around with your fingers. Keep going until all the coconut is green.

- When the biscuits are cold, cover one side of each tree in icing (except for the trunk), using a spatula. Hold the tree by its trunk and dip it into the green coconut.

- Place the dragees on your Christmas trees like baubles, then put the star on top of your large tree!

To put the biscuits and cake together

- Once you've iced the top of your cake, gently press your decorated biscuits into the icing, so they stick to the surface. I've put the big tree in the centre and the smaller ones around it, but you can use whatever pattern you like.

Hooray for
OUT OF SCHOOL

Holly lived on a small street, in a small house that was beside an even smaller corner shop. Holly's Auntie Isabella owned the shop. It was the kind of shop where nothing made sense – cans of beans were next to the wrapping paper and cinnamon was next to the toilet roll.

Auntie Isabella was eighty-one, she loved ballroom dancing and she wasn't Holly's actual real-life aunt.

"Everyone in the playground thinks I'm young enough to be your aunty," she would say proudly, as she flamenco-danced across the floor of the tiny shop to the till. She still wore the flouncy dresses from her ballroom-dancing days.

"Are you from Spain, Auntie Isabella?" Holly asked one day, as she neatened the mints and then the turkey foil. Holly spent every evening with Auntie Isabella because Holly's parents had to work late. They worked so hard and were always so busy, and Holly worried about how tired they looked all the time.

She always wished she could do more to help them.

"I go every summer for two weeks, so I reckon that makes me almost Spanish," Auntie Isabella replied. "Did I mention the food there is fab?" She smacked her lips and gave Holly 50p to put in her piggy bank, just because.

Holly's mum and dad were not just her mum and dad, they were the headmistress and the caretaker of Mulberry Primary School. Holly got to see her mum and dad at school all day, which she loved. She'd always get a special wink from her dad and a special smile from her mum, and she found out about all the things that were happening at school before the other pupils. That made her feel special, but she still missed her parents in the evenings.

That morning, as Holly and her parents walked to school, Holly noticed that they looked more tired than normal, but before she could worry too much, her mum asked what the date was. Holly thought for a minute, then realised – it was the first of December!

"And what does that mean, Holly?" Dad asked, stifling a yawn.

"Countdown to Hooray for Out of School!" Holly shouted and punched the air. It was her favourite time of year, when everyone at Mulberry Primary made advent calendars and counted down to the

Hooray for Out of School fair on the last day of term. There would be rides, real reindeer, Santa's Grotto, roasted chestnuts, hot dogs and so much more. Holly could not wait.

After school, Auntie Isabella and Holly cha-cha-cha-ed all the way home.

"1, 2 ... 1, 2, 3!" Auntie Isabella sang.

But Holly didn't join in with the singing. She was still thinking about her parents and how she could try and make things easier for them.

"Auntie Isabella, will you help me with something?" she asked.

"Anything and everything your heart desires," Auntie Isabella replied and squeezed Holly's hand tight. "As long as we can dance while we do it!"

December rushed by and the Mulberry Primary pupils happily ticked off the dates on their advent calendars. Finally, the Hooray for Out of School fair arrived. Holly's mum and dad walked around the fair, making sure everything was running smoothly, while Holly walked around with Auntie Isabella.

"Mum?" Holly tugged at her mum's jacket. "I'm going to go back to Auntie Isabella's shop now, if that's okay?"

"Are you sure? But the fair's only just begun – it's your favourite day of the year!" her mum said, surprised.

"I've ... um ... I've got things to do!" Holly blurted, and with a sneaky grin at Auntie Isabella, made a dash for the door. Auntie Isabella pirouetted after her, finishing off with a leap and jazz hands for good measure.

Back at the shop, they gathered ingredients from the shelves:

tomatoes, cheese, peppers, onions and lots more. All the ingredients for a recipe Auntie Isabella had found in Spain.

Holly handed over an envelope containing all the 50ps Auntie Isabella had given her.

Auntie Isabella smiled at her proudly. "What a nice thing to do, Holly. But, you shouldn't have to pay for anything here, so I will just pop it into the charity box instead."

They worked fast and hard all evening to make a feast. And when Mum and Dad arrived to pick Holly up, weary after the fair and even more weary at the thought of having to cook dinner later, a treat met their eyes.

"Welcome to the best Hooray for Out of School day ever," Holly announced. "And now, dinner is served. Crashed eggs, sweet cheese and chive cakes, and fruit skewers."

Mum and Dad covered Holly with kisses for her help and gratefully sank into their chairs. Auntie Isabella was so happy she did the splits.

"Hooray for out of school!" they all cheered, then everyone tucked right in.

SWEET CHEESE AND CHIVE CAKES

You could enjoy these warm, buttery cheese and chive cakes on their own, but they are also the perfect accompaniment to the yummy crashed eggs on the next page. However you choose to eat them, they won't last long!

Makes 4

Ingredients

50g unsalted butter, softened, plus 30g
    for frying

250g plain flour, plus extra for the work
    surface

½ tsp fast action dried yeast

½ tsp salt

20g caster sugar

50g Red Leicester cheese, finely grated

10g chives, finely chopped

120ml whole milk, warmed

5 tbsp olive oil, plus extra
    for oiling

1 medium egg

Method

- Add the 50g of butter and the flour to a bowl and rub together with the tips of your fingers until the mixture resembles breadcrumbs.

- Add the yeast to one side of the bowl. Add the salt to the other side.

- Now add the sugar, cheese and chives. Using a palette knife, give everything a good mix.

- Add the warmed milk to a jug and crack the egg in. Whisk lightly to combine.

- Make a well in the dry ingredients and pour in the wet ingredients, along with the oil. Use a palette knife and mix together well.

- Sprinkle flour on the work surface and knead the dough for 10 minutes. The mixture will be quite sticky, but the more you knead it, the smoother it will become.

- Lightly oil the inside of a clean bowl. Put the dough in the bowl and cover with a clean tea towel. Set aside for 30 minutes. If you are making the crashed eggs, now's a good time to start preparing them!

- After 30 minutes, remove the dough from the bowl. Lightly oil both the work surface and your hands, then roll the dough into a sausage shape.

- Cut the 'sausage' into eight equal chunks. Roll each chunk into a ball then flatten down to approximately 1cm thick using the palm of your hand.

- Melt the 30g of butter in a large non-stick frying pan. Take four of the cakes, flatten again, then add them to the pan.

- Fry over a medium to low heat for 3–4 minutes on each side, or until golden brown and cooked through.

- Remove with a spatula and place on kitchen towel to remove any excess butter. Keep warm while you fry the rest of the cakes.

- Serve warm with the crashed eggs.

CRASHED EGGS

If one of your children is confident with chopping, this is a great recipe for them to try. The chunky tomato base is full of peppers, onions and sausages, and they all need chopping up! Serve with the Sweet Cheese and Chive Cakes for the perfect taste combination.

Serves 4

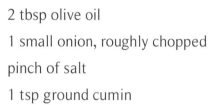

Ingredients

2 tbsp olive oil

1 small onion, roughly chopped

pinch of salt

1 tsp ground cumin

6 vegetarian sausages, chopped into
   1cm slices (see tip)

½ yellow pepper, roughly chopped

2 ripe tomatoes, cubed

1 tsp caster sugar

500g passata

2 tbsp flat leaf parsley, roughly chopped

4 large eggs

Method

- Place a medium non-stick sauté pan on a medium heat. Add the oil, onion, salt and cumin. Cook the onions for 2 minutes until they have softened slightly.

- Add the chopped sausages and cook for 5–7 minutes until they are cooked through.

- Add the yellow pepper, tomatoes, sugar and passata. Cook for 10 minutes until the mixture thickens.

- Make four wells in the mixture and gently crack an egg into each well. Cover and leave to cook on a low heat for 5 minutes.

- Sprinkle the parsley over the cooked eggs. Serve in bowls with the Cheese and Chive Cakes on the side.

NADIYA'S TIP
You can use meat sausages if you prefer. If you do, add the sausages with a little oil to the pan first, cook for 10 minutes or until golden all over, then add the onion, salt and cumin and cook for another 2-3 minutes.

FRUIT SKEWERS

Fruit skewers are a simple and easy dessert to make. You might like to use seasonal fruit, so perhaps apples and pears in the winter, or plums in the autumn. I've chosen to use tropical fruit this time, as I think Auntie Isabella would approve!

Makes 4

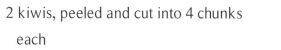

Ingredients

2 kiwis, peeled and cut into 4 chunks
  each

12 pineapple chunks (tinned
  or fresh)

1 large banana, peeled and cut into
  8 chunky slices

50g milk chocolate

25g roasted chopped hazelnuts

You will also need

4 x wooden skewers

Method

🍂 Skewer the fruit in whatever pattern you want. I like all my skewers to look the same.

🍂 Lay the skewers flat on a plate.

🍂 Melt the chocolate in a microwave or in an ovenproof bowl set over a pan of simmering water.

🍂 Using a teaspoon, drizzle the melted chocolate over the skewers in long strokes.

🍂 Sprinkle with the hazelnuts. Turn the skewers over and repeat the drizzling and the sprinkling to coat both sides.

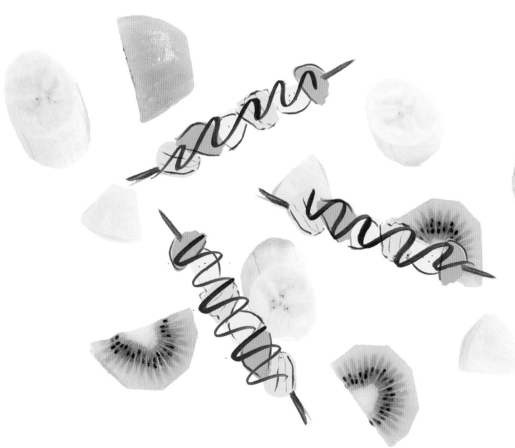

NADIYA'S TIP
If you are preparing the fruit in advance, put all the chopped fruit in a bowl before you skewer it. Squeeze lemon juice over it and give it all a gentle stir. This will stop the fruit from browning.

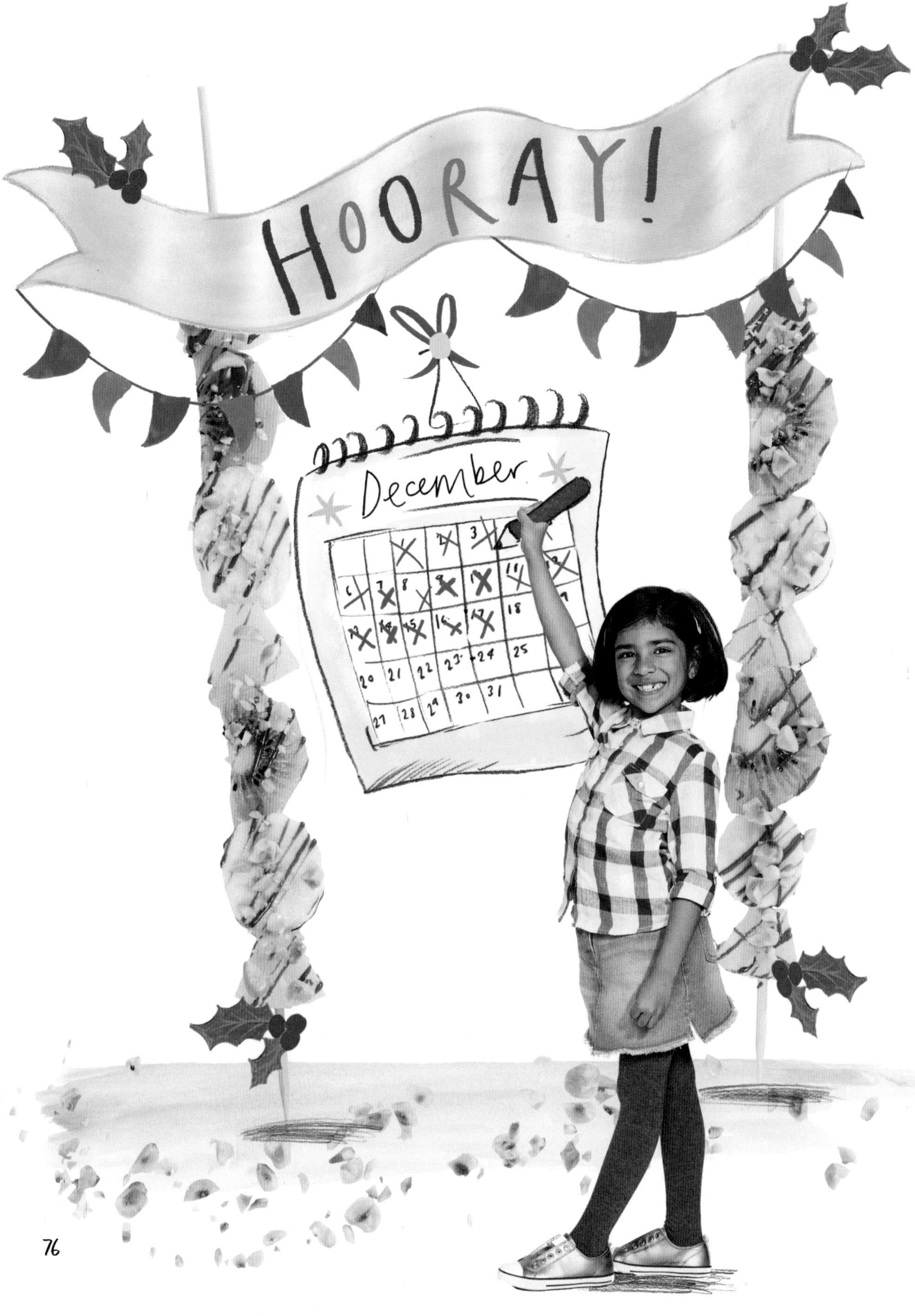
HOORAY!
December

The Elves and the
CHOUX MAKER

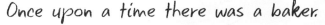

Once upon a time there was a baker. He wasn't any old baker, he made the best choux pastry in the whole wide world. His choux was lighter, crispier and airier than any other baker could make, and people flocked to his bakery from far away just to get a taste.

He made long choux, short choux, round choux and even rounder choux. They were filled with every kind of filling and topped with every kind of topping you could ever dream of. But even though he was the best choux maker around, he was also the meanest. There were no free samples going at his bakery – not even at Christmas.

The baker's wife was quite the opposite. She was cheery and caring, and despite her husband's meanness, the kind-hearted woman still loved him very much. She would spend every afternoon in their flat above the shop, cooking the baker his favourite salmon curry for dinner.

One chilly December evening, as the baker was shutting up his shop for the night, a thin, scruffy man came into the bakery.

"I am looking for the famous baker who makes the world's best ch ... ch ... Sorry, how do you say it?"

"Choux. Like you'd say 'shoe'," the baker replied, sharply. He wanted to get home to his curry. "And that would be me you're looking for."

"Oh, great," said the man. "I don't have any money, but I am awfully hungry. I don't suppose you have a choux you could spare? Maybe I could take a couple for my friends at the shelter, if you are throwing out the leftovers?"

"Spare? You can only have the best choux in the land if you pay for it!" the baker growled, even though he knew he was just about to throw out the leftovers from the day. "If you don't have any money, go away, back to the shelter, where you belong!"

The baker pushed the man out of his shop and slammed the door.

79

Later that night, after the baker had finished his curry, his wife put on her coat and scarf.

"Where are you going?" he asked her.

"I cooked some extra curry for the people in the shelter. I'm going to drop it off," she answered.

"I don't know why you waste your time," he said, tutting.

"Because sometimes, people just need some kindness and a smile," she replied, and left him to be grumpy on his own.

It wasn't long before the baker, his belly full of the day's choux and a tasty portion of his wife's extraordinary salmon curry, fell fast asleep.

Meanwhile, downstairs in the bakery, something curious was going on. A gang of elves were sitting on the countertop, looking a bit puzzled.

"Are you sure this is the right place?" said one elf to another. "I mean, we're here to make shoes, right?"

"Yeah, that's what that pixie said, back at the crossroads,"

the other elf said. "World's Best Shoe Maker ..."

These little elves worked tirelessly to make shoes for those who didn't have any, especially over the winter when the cold would bite your toes.

"But where's the leather, or the tacks, or the laces?" a third elf asked.

"I haven't found any of that," said another elf from inside a cupboard. "But I have found butter, water, eggs and flour ... oh, and here's the World's Best Shoe Maker's instructions."

The elves followed the instructions as closely as they could, but as they took their shoes out of the oven, they were still perplexed.

"Do you think this is a new trend we don't know about?" said the first elf, trying on one of the freshly made shoes. They definitely kept his feet warm. He stood up to test them out on a walk, but he accidentally knocked a baking tray off of the countertop, sending it clanging to the floor.

The baker woke with a start and rushed downstairs, into the shop. "What are you doing in my bakery?" he shouted.

"Bakery?" the elves squeaked in surprise. "Isn't this the place where the best shoes in the world are made?"

"CHOUX!" the baker bellowed. "C. H. O. U. X! Sounds the same as 'shoe.'"

Then the baker took a proper look at the elves with choux buns on their feet instead of shoes, and burst out laughing at the sight. He had not laughed in years. It felt good.

The elves joined in with the laughter, but it soon turned to worry.

"We have made all of this pastry, but now it's only going to go to waste ..." one elf wailed. "We are meant to be helping people, not wasting food."

The baker had an idea. He pointed at the elves. "You prick holes on the base of every choux and line them up, I will make a filling and a topping and then we can do something really special with them."

Back at the shelter, the baker's wife opened the door and gasped. Standing on the doorstep was her husband, accompanied by a gang of grinning elves, their arms piled high with cake boxes.

"Thought your friends here might like dessert," the baker said, gruffly.

The baker's wife pulled her husband into a huge hug, then they sang carols and served the best choux buns to all the hungry tummies at the shelter.

The choux maker wasn't just the best choux maker in the world, he was now the happiest choux maker in the world, too.

BAKEWELL CHOUX ÉCLAIRS

'Choux' might be a bit tricky to pronounce (it sounds just the same as the word 'shoe'), but it's so much fun to make. This recipe is a cross between a long choux bun and a bakewell tart. I'd recommend eating them and not wearing them, though!

Makes 12-14

Ingredients

For the pastry

50g unsalted butter, cold and cubed, plus
   extra for greasing
150ml water
65g plain flour, sifted
2 eggs, beaten

For the cherry cream

300ml double cream
2 tbsp cherry jam

For the topping

125g icing sugar, sifted
2 tbsp water
½ tsp almond extract
20g toasted flaked
   almonds (see tip)

Method

- Preheat the oven to 200°C fan/gas mark 7. Lightly grease two baking trays with butter.

- Put the butter and water in a small saucepan over a medium heat. Bring to the boil, making sure all the butter has melted. Don't let it bubble for too long – you don't want too much water to evaporate as then the choux won't be the right consistency.

- Take it off the heat and add the flour, making sure you stir it quickly to combine. The mixture should be a thick paste that comes away from the sides of the pan. Let the pan cool for a few minutes.

- Gradually add the beaten egg, mixing with a wooden spoon the whole time. Beat the mixture hard to make sure all the egg is incorporated and it turns into a smooth batter.

- Put the mixture into a piping bag, or, if you don't have one, into a large zip-lock food bag. Snip off one corner of the food bag to make a hole about 1.5cm wide.

- Pipe the mixture straight onto the baking trays in long straight lines about 8cm long. Keep going until the bag is empty.

- Wet your fingertips slightly, then smooth off any sharp points. This will stop these bits burning.

- Bake in the oven for 18–20 minutes, until golden brown and crisp. Remove the trays from the oven and leave the choux éclairs to cool on a wire rack.

- Meanwhile, make the cherry cream filling. First, whip the cream into soft peaks. Add the jam and stir it in gently so you get ripples of colour.

- Make a long slit on the underside of each éclair, making sure not to go all of the way through to the top.

- Fit a nozzle to a clean piping bag (or snip a 1.5cm hole in a fresh zip-lock bag) and fill the bag with the cherry cream.

- Pipe cream inside the slit in each éclair.

- Mix the icing sugar with the water and almond extract in a bowl until you have a smooth paste. Spoon the icing along the top of each éclair and sprinkle on a few toasted almonds.

NADIYA'S TIP
If you can't find toasted flaked almonds in the shops, you can toast them yourself. Just toss them in a dry pan over a medium heat for 2-3 minutes, until golden brown and smelling toasty!

LEMON SHORTCAKE CHOUX BUNS

There are all sorts of flavours that you can add to choux. Tangy lemon will cut through the sweetness of the icing and the crunch of the biscuit topping will add an interesting texture in your mouth. Which choux will be your favourite?

Makes 14

Ingredients

For the pastry

50g unsalted butter, cold and cubed, plus extra for greasing

150ml water

65g plain flour, sifted

2 eggs, beaten

For the lemon cream

300ml double cream

2 tbsp lemon curd

grated zest of 1 lemon (use the juice for the icing)

For the topping

120g icing sugar, sifted

2 tbsp lemon juice

30g shortbread biscuits, roughly crushed

Method

- Preheat the oven to 200°C fan/gas mark 7. Lightly grease two baking trays with butter.

- Put the butter and water in a small saucepan over a medium heat. Bring to the boil, making sure all the butter has melted. Don't let it bubble for too long – you don't want too much water to evaporate as then the choux won't be the right consistency.

- Take it off the heat and add the flour, making sure you stir it quickly to combine. The mixture should be a thick paste that comes away from the sides of the pan. Let the pan cool for a few minutes.

- Gradually add the beaten egg, mixing with a wooden spoon the whole time. Beat the mixture hard to make sure all the egg is incorporated and it turns into a smooth batter.

- Put the mixture into a piping bag, or, if you don't have one, into a large zip-lock food bag. Snip off the point of the food bag to make a hole about 1.5cm wide.

- Pipe 14 mounds straight on to the baking trays.

- Wet your fingertips slightly, then smooth off any sharp points. This will stop these bits burning.

- Bake in the oven for 18–20 minutes, until golden brown and crisp. Remove the trays from the oven and leave the choux buns to cool on a wire rack.

- Meanwhile, make the lemon cream filling. First, whip the cream into soft peaks. Add the lemon curd and lemon zest and stir it in gently so you get ripples of colour.

- Make a deep slit on the underside of each bun, making sure not to go all of the way through to the top.

- Fit a nozzle to a clean piping bag (or snip a 1.5cm hole in a fresh zip-lock bag), and fill the bag with the lemon cream.

- Pipe cream inside the slit in each bun.

- Mix the icing sugar and lemon juice in a bowl until you have a smooth paste. Spoon the icing on top of each bun and sprinkle with the crushed shortbread.

SALMON AND GREEN BEAN CURRY

This is a delicious curry with lots of lovely spices to warm you from the inside out. It's easy to make and even easier to eat.

Serves 4

Ingredients

3 tbsp olive oil

3 garlic cloves, peeled and crushed

10g fresh ginger, peeled and finely grated

1 small onion, chopped

¼ tsp salt

1 tsp tomato purée

1 small tomato, chopped

½ tsp turmeric

2 tsp garam masala

400ml water

170g green beans, trimmed and chopped into 2.5cm pieces

450g salmon, skin removed, chopped into chunks

handful of fresh coriander, roughly chopped

Method

~ Put the oil, garlic, ginger, onion and salt in a medium non-stick saucepan. Cook for about 5 minutes on a medium heat, until the onions have softened.

~ Add the tomato purée, chopped tomato, turmeric and garam masala and cook for another minute.

~ Add half the water and let it cook down until most of the moisture has evaporated.

~ Add the rest of the water and the green beans, then cook for 5 minutes before adding the salmon. Cover and cook for 5 minutes on a medium heat.

~ Take the pan off the heat and stir in the coriander.

~ Serve with brown rice.

It was Thursday. Secretly, Benji didn't like Thursdays all that much. He preferred Wednesdays, because he had gymnastics after school on Wednesday.

On Thursdays, Benji's mum went to the supermarket to do shopping for the old folk at the retirement home. And Benji had to go too. He would rather be doing cartwheels on a Thursday. And handstands, and headstands, and anything else that meant he could be upside down.

"No dawdling after school today. Come straight out after the bell," his mum said. "We're shopping for Cora, Tim and Phyllis."

So Benji rushed out of school as soon as the bell sounded, just as his mum had asked. It was December, so the sun was going down as they walked to the retirement home.

One by one, lights started to twinkle in people's windows. Some were white, some were colourful. Some just shone and others flashed on and off. It made the dark street beautiful. Benji felt so happy, he wanted to do a cartwheel. But the road was wet, so he didn't.

When they got to the retirement home, Cora, Tim and Phyllis were sat around a table playing a board game and having tea and biscuits. They handed over their shopping lists to Benji's mum, but she didn't really need them. The old folks bought the same things, every single Thursday.

"Same as usual then!" said mum, cheerily. "We'll see you shortly."

When Benji and Mum got to the supermarket, Mum handed Benji the lists. "It makes me so proud that you help me with the shopping, Benji, and you never complain. Shall we play a game to make it a bit more fun today?"

Benji nodded. He'd still rather be practising handstands but it made him feel good to make his mum proud.

"Right then. I'll call a name and a number, and you see if you can tell me what we need to find on the shelves. Ready ...? Cora! Two!"

"Hmmm. That'll be ... bananas!" Benji said, pleased with himself for his quick thinking.

But Mum was studying Cora's list. "Hang on," she said. "This is odd. It says nutmeg."

"Must be a mistake, Mum," Benji said. "But this is fun! Try me with another, and I will go and find it."

Mum looked up and smiled. "Let's try Tim's list then. Four!"

Benji knew the answer straightaway. "Milk!"

"Er, no. It says tinned peaches." Mum looked really puzzled now. "Well, if this is what they want, then this is what we will get."

So Benji and his mum went around the shelves together, looking for the unusual shopping. Benji asked questions about the food he had never heard of before, like polenta and sour cherries, and Mum told him what they were. Benji was enjoying himself so much he didn't think about cartwheeling once.

When Benji and Mum got back to the retirement home, they put the shopping into the cupboards, like they did every week. Cora, Tim and Phyllis normally insisted that they stay for a game of snakes and ladders and a cup of tea, but this afternoon the old folks made excuses.

"I'm so tired!" said Cora.

"I need to tidy my sock drawer," said Tim.

"I need to ... um ... er ... Oh, would you look at that! It's dark outside," said Phyllis. "You'd better get going."

So Benji and Mum said goodbye and headed home for their tea.

When next Thursday came, it was time for another trip to the supermarket after school. Benji and his mum went into the home. Cora, Tim and Phyllis were in their usual spot, but instead of a board game, there was something else sitting on the table.

Phyllis stood up and cleared her throat. "We wanted to say thank you for everything you do for us."

"And we heard that you love doing handstands, Benji," Cora said.

"So we made you both an upside-down cake!" Tim said. "That's why we wanted different things on our shopping lists last week."

Mum and Benji gave their friends a happy hug and while his mum went to get plates, Benji showed the old folks his best handstand. They all had a slice of upside-down cake, and smiled at the Christmas lights, twinkling in the retirement home windows.

PEACH AND CHERRY UPSIDE-DOWN CAKE

I like the combination of squidgy, sweet peaches and sour cherries in my upside-down cake, but you can use any tinned soft fruits that you have at home. The best bit is when you turn the cake upside down and discover all the colourful fruit. It's a bit like opening a present and seeing what treats are inside!

Serves 10-12

Ingredients

200g tinned sliced peaches, drained (keep the syrup for the drizzle)

50g dried sour cherries

220g polenta

80g plain flour, sifted

1 tsp bicarbonate of soda

1 tsp ground nutmeg

200g unsalted butter, softened

140g runny honey

grated zest of 1 lemon (use the juice for the drizzle)

medium eggs, lightly beaten

For the drizzle

75g caster sugar

juice of 1 lemon

syrup from the tinned peaches

Method

🍒 Preheat the oven to 150°C fan/gas mark 3. Grease the base of a 900g loaf tin and line with baking paper.

🍒 Line the base of the tin with peaches, one by one, until it is completely covered. Place cherries in the gaps until you have used them all up.

🍒 Mix the polenta, flour, bicarbonate of soda and nutmeg in a small bowl.

🍒 In a separate large bowl, beat the butter and honey until light and fluffy. Add the lemon zest and eggs and mix together.

🍒 Add the dry ingredients to the wet ingredients and give it all a really good stir.

🍒 Pour the mixture into the tin, on top of the peaches and cherries. Bake for for 1 hour and 15 minutes. Check the cake is baked by inserting a skewer into the middle. If the skewer comes out clean, the cake's ready.

🍒 Remove from the oven and leave to cool in the tin for 30 minutes before turning out.

VANILLA CUSTARD

A simple vanilla custard can make an already yummy cake even yummier! This custard goes really well with most cakes, and sometimes I just eat a bowl of it all on its own. Yum!

Serves 12

Ingredients

3 large egg yolks

4 tsp cornflour

25g caster sugar

1 tsp vanilla extract

600ml whole milk

Method

- Whisk the egg yolks, cornflour, sugar and vanilla in a bowl until combined.

- Put the milk in a medium pan over a medium heat.

- Before the milk reaches boiling point, pour it slowly over the egg mixture, making sure you whisk the whole time.

- Once all the milk is added, pour the mixture back into the pan over a low heat.

- Keep stirring until the mixture thickens. You will know it is ready when it coats the back of your spoon.

- Take off the heat, pour into a jug and it is ready to serve.

NADIYA'S TIP
If the custard splits, take it off the heat immediately and blend in a food processor to bring the custard back together. Pour into a jug and place the jug in a bowl of ice to cool quickly.

Jack

FROST

There was a young boy called Jako. He was the kind of boy who spent all day, every day, outside. From the moment he woke up to the time he went to bed, he spent it outside. And Jako loved the snow, the frost, the cold that made the tip of his nose go pink – Jako loved it all. When he wasn't chilly, he felt very strange indeed.

His dad said it was because his name was Frost – Jako Frost Junior. Luckily, Jako and his dad, Jako Frost Senior, lived in Finland, where it was very cold.

When Dad took Jako on holiday, they went to Austria, to Sweden, to Alaska. They loved to go anywhere it snowed.

Every winter, Jako's grandparents would come and stay. They were from Scotland, and Jako looked forward to seeing them for weeks and weeks before they arrived.

One year, Jako's dad, Jako Senior, told him they would be going to Scotland for the winter instead. "It can get pretty cold there, Jako Junior. You mustn't worry."

"But Dad, will there be snow?" Jako asked.

"There seems to be snow wherever you go," Dad said.

When they arrived in Scotland, Jako Junior and Jako Senior walked through the airport – there were Granny and Grandpa! But Jako Junior was worried.

"What's the matter?" asked Granny, after she'd wrapped him up in a big squishy hug.

"Where's the snow, Granny? Dad said there's always snow, wherever I go. But I couldn't see any from the windows of the plane. And it's not very cold right now."

"You never know when it will snow," Granny reassured him.

When they got home, Jako helped his grandpa decorate the Christmas tree. He hung the stockings, he helped wrap presents, he even helped Granny clean the oven. Now and again he snuck a look outside, but there was still no sign of snow. Jako Frost simply didn't feel right.

Later, Granny found Jako curled up in a corner, reading a book about snowmen. She produced an apron for Jako from behind her back.

"I can't make it snow outside, but how do you fancy making a little snow inside?" Granny asked.

Jako's eyes lit up. "Yes please!" he said.

"I hoped you'd say that," Granny replied.

They spent a wonderful afternoon giggling and making a mess in the kitchen. As Jako sieved great clouds of icing sugar over the oopsie doopsie breads, he happily told Granny it looked a bit like powdery snow.

"Why don't you wish for snow in the garden, Jako?" Granny replied. "You never know what might happen …"

Jako screwed his eyes up tight and wished as hard as he could.

Next was Grandpa's favourite, the Queen of Puddings. Jako piped the fluffy meringue on top, and he took care to make the snowy mountains on top of the pudding as high as he could.

It was almost as good as climbing to the top of a real snowy mountain.

"Where's Grandpa?" Jako asked, when the pudding finally came out of the oven. "He should have the first slice."

"He's in the garden, Jako," Granny replied. "Before we cut him a slice, how about we go to the window and you make your wish again? Close your eyes nice and tight and wish really hard. Just in case."

Jako closed his eyes really tight, and Granny steered him towards the window.

"Now, open them," she said, quietly.

Jako could have jumped for joy. Great flurries of beautiful white snow were falling outside. Grandpa and Dad were standing beside a snow machine, grinning from ear to ear at the sight of Jako's happy face.

Jako played outside in the snow until the sun came down. Then he settled down with his family to tuck into oopsie doopsie snow bread, and a big bowl of pudding.

Jako Frost Junior felt right again.

OOPSIE DOOPSIE SNOW BREAD

Just like Jack Frost, I love the snow. I don't have a snow machine in my garden, but I can make it snow indoors with a batch of my own Oopsie Doopsie Snow Bread! This is one of the easiest breads you will ever make, although it'll need a bit of welly with the whisk.

Makes 6

Ingredients

3 large eggs

120g full-fat cream cheese

¼ tsp salt

2 tbsp self-raising flour, sifted

1 tsp baking powder

4 tsp sesame seeds

1–2 tbsp icing sugar, sifted

Method

※ Preheat the oven to 160°C fan/gas mark 4. Line two baking trays with baking paper.

※ Separate the eggs into yolks and whites in two large bowls.

※ Add the cream cheese to the bowl with the egg yolks and whisk until all the lumps have gone. Set aside.

※ Add the salt to the bowl with the egg whites and whisk to stiff peaks.

※ Add the egg whites to the egg yolks mixture and fold it through using a metal spoon. Don't worry if it is a bit lumpy at this stage!

※ Fold in the flour and baking powder, making sure you don't overwork the mixture.

※ Spoon the mixture onto the baking trays in six mounds.

※ Sprinkle the top of each mound with sesame seeds.

※ Bake for 20–25 minutes until the mounds are golden brown.

※ Make it snow by sifting the icing sugar on top!

QUEEN OF PUDDINGS

This wintry dessert has so many delicious layers to delve through – creamy custard, tangy jam and snowy meringue mountain peaks. You can show off your layers if you make it in a see-through dish.

Serves 6-8

Ingredients

For the custard layer

25g unsalted butter, plus extra
  for greasing

600ml whole milk

1 tsp vanilla extract

3 large egg yolks (save the whites for
  the meringues)

50g caster sugar

100g fresh white breadcrumbs

For the jam layer

6 tbsp smooth strawberry jam

For the meringue layer

3 egg whites

175g caster sugar

Method

❋ Preheat the oven to 150°C fan/gas mark 3. Grease a 1.4-litre ovenproof dish.

❋ Find a roasting tray large enough for the dish to fit in and set aside.

❋ Put the butter, milk and vanilla in a medium saucepan on a medium heat and bring the mixture to a gentle simmer.

❋ Whisk the egg yolks and sugar in a bowl until pale and light.

❋ Now add the hot milk to the egg mixture, making sure you stir it all the time.

❋ Sprinkle the breadcrumbs over the base of the greased dish. Pour the milk and egg mixture over the top.

❋ Sit the dish inside the roasting tray and pour boiling water into the roasting tray until the water is halfway up the outside of the dish.

❋ Put the tray into the oven and bake for 25–30 minutes.

❋ When baked, take the tray out of the oven and remove the dish. Lower the oven temperature to 130°C fan/gas mark 2.

❋ Warm the jam in a small pan or in the microwave, just enough to loosen.

❋ For the meringue, add the egg whites to a bowl and whisk until the mixture comes to soft peaks. Then add the sugar 1 tablespoon at a time and continue whisking. The meringue will be ready when there are stiff peaks and the mixture is glossy.

❋ Spoon the meringue mixture into a piping bag (see tip).

❋ Pour the jam all over the baked custard and gently spread into a thin, even layer.

❋ Pipe large peaks of meringue on top of the jam and bake the pudding in the oven for 25–30 minutes.

❋ Serve immediately.

NADIYA'S TIP

If you don't have a piping bag to add the meringue, you could just use a spoon. Try and bring the mixture into nice peaks if you can, but don't worry if you can't – the pudding will taste just as delicious!

Dress Down to
DRESS UP

It was the week before the Christmas Party at school and all the children were giddy with excitement. There was always a Secret Santa and, best of all, they got to dress down, out of their school uniform. The children knew that their uniform was what made their school look so neat and tidy. But they did love dressing down to dress up.

This year, the dressing-up theme was animals. First, everyone decided what animal they were going to dress down to dress up as. They wrote that animal's name on a piece of paper and put it in a Santa's hat, then the teacher walked around with the hat so everyone could pick a piece of paper out. You wouldn't know who had chosen each animal, but that was who you had to bring a Secret Santa treat for. It made the party a bit crazy but so much more fun!

"Everyone take a box," the teacher called out, holding up a pile of plain cardboard boxes. "You can decorate it and fill it with something delicious your animal friend might like to eat. And remember what we've been learning this month ... What's the festive season for?"

"CARING AND SHARING!" the children chorused, and they scurried out of school, ready to think up ideas to make their unknown animal friend smile.

A week passed, and it was party day. Everyone had dressed down to dress up. The teacher pushed the tables and chairs back so the kids could mingle and look for the animal that their box was for.

"I'm looking for a magpie!" one little girl dressed up as a cat said. "I covered my box in sequins and my biscuits in edible glitter because magpies like sparkly things!" And off she went to hunt for her magpie.

"Hey, Ted the fruit bat!" a boy dressed as a chicken called across the room. "I've got cranberry and white chocolate shortbread for you! It's soooo good."

"I've got squashed fly cupcakes for a frog," said another child.

Andy the frog didn't look too excited to hear that, and hid in Library Corner.

"Maisie the rabbit, here is your box," the teacher said. She was dressed as an elephant. There were carrots painted all over the sides of the box.

113

Maisie opened it immediately and inside were veggie swirls, bursting with a rabbit's favourite, carrots, and lots of other colourful vegetables besides. Maisie was thrilled with her Secret Santa.

Soon, everyone had a box and a treat to take home. Everyone apart from one very sad little donkey.

Chloe the donkey didn't have a box because one of the children in the class had tummy ache and hadn't come into school that day. Poor Chloe felt so left out.

Then, before the teacher realised what was going on, every one of the children in the class made a line in front of Chloe, with Maisie the rabbit right at the front.

"Don't cry, Chloe," Maisie said. *"Donkeys love carrots as much as bunnies do, so here's one of my carroty veggie swirls just for you."*

"And here's one of my cranberry and white chocolate shortbreads," said Ted the fruit bat, who was next in line. "I think donkeys like cranberries, don't they?"

And, one by one, the children gave Chloe the donkey a treat from their box. The teacher quickly wrapped a spare box with Christmas paper and before long, Chloe had a mega treat all of her own to go home with.

The teacher was very proud that her class had listened to everything she'd said that month, and were doing the best Christmas sharing and caring she had ever seen.

CRANBERRY AND WHITE CHOCOLATE SHORTBREAD

These biscuits can be a real team effort. Younger children can enjoy rolling the little balls and coating them in sugar, and older children can give it some welly creaming the butter and sugar. Everyone can get their hands in and get messy!

Makes 18

Ingredients

125g unsalted butter, softened

55g caster sugar, plus 20g for rolling

1 tsp vanilla extract

180g plain flour

60g white chocolate, finely chopped or chips

60g dried cranberries

Method

Preheat the oven to 170°C fan/gas mark 5. Line two baking trays with baking paper.

Cream the butter and the 55g of sugar in a large bowl until light and fluffy. Add the vanilla extract and mix well.

Add the flour and mix to make a smooth dough.

Add in the chocolate and cranberries, stirring until they are evenly spread throughout the dough.

Pour the 20g of sugar for rolling into a shallow dish.

Separate the dough into 18 small balls. Dip and roll each ball in the extra sugar so they are completely coated. Place the balls on the trays, spaced about an inch apart.

Bake for 20 minutes, until they are golden brown.

Remove from the oven and leave the biscuits to cool on the tray for 15 minutes, then transfer them to a wire rack to cool completely.

VEGGIE SWIRLS

This is a great recipe to challenge older kids, while younger kids can have a go at the accompanying Sour Cream and Chive Dip over the page. You could tuck into these gorgeous doughy swirls warm out of the oven or as a snack later when cooled down.

Makes 8

Ingredients

For the filling

20g unsalted butter

1 red onion, chopped

1 tsp curry powder

130g frozen mixed vegetables (e.g. peas, green beans, sweetcorn, carrots)

100g Cheddar cheese, grated

salt and pepper

1 tsp curry powder

100g unsalted butter

200ml whole milk

2 egg yolks

For the dough

400g self-raising flour, plus extra for the work surface

pinch of salt

2 tbsp caster sugar

Method

- Preheat the oven to 160°C fan/gas mark 4. Grease a 22cm round, loose-bottomed cake tin and line with baking paper.

- Put the butter in a non-stick saucepan and melt over a medium heat.

- Add the onion and season with salt and pepper to taste. Cook the onions for a few minutes, until soft.

- Add the curry powder and cook for 1 minute.

- Add the frozen vegetables and cook for a further 10 minutes on a medium heat, until the vegetables are soft.

- Remove from the heat and blitz to a chunky paste in a food processor. You can add a little trickle of water if necessary to help it blend.

  Transfer to a bowl and leave to cool down completely.

- Meanwhile, get started on the dough. Mix the flour, salt, sugar and and curry powder in a bowl until combined.

- Melt the butter in a small saucepan over a low heat.

- Pour the melted butter into a jug, add the milk and egg yolks, and beat lightly.

- Make a well in the centre of the dry ingredients and pour in the wet ingredients, making sure to hold back a bit of the liquid for glazing. Bring the dough together to a smooth ball with your hands.

- Tip the dough on to a floured surface, and roll it out to a rectangle about 30x25cm.

- Spread the cool vegetable mixture all over the dough. Sprinkle with the cheese.

- Starting from the long edge closest to you, roll the dough up tightly, like a Swiss roll, until you have a long sausage.

- Cut the sausage into eight equal pieces, using a sharp knife.

- Turning the pieces on their side so you can see the swirls, place them in the cake tin in a ring pattern. Make sure they are all touching if you want something you can tear and share. Alternatively, you can bake them as individual swirls on a baking tray.

- Brush the top of the swirls with the leftover liquid and bake for 30–40 minutes, until golden brown.

- Remove from the oven and leave in the tin for at least 30 minutes before serving with the Sour Cream and Chive Dip.

SOUR CREAM AND CHIVE DIP

Ingredients

150ml soured cream

2 tbsp chives, chopped

grated zest of 1 lemon

Method

- Put the soured cream in a small cereal bowl. Sprinkle on the chives and the lemon zest.

- Give all the ingredients a good stir, until the chives and the lemon zest are nicely distributed throughout.

- Serve with your veggie swirls, or vegetable sticks to dip!

The
NUTCRACKER

It was way past their bedtime, but Polly and Peter were wide awake. Uncle Sid was coming to visit and they loved Uncle Sid so much. He would give them piggy-back rides and do silly voices when he read them stories, and he always brought them a special present. Uncle Sid's presents were more special than any other presents because he didn't just go to the shop and pay for toys, he made them with his own hands. Last Christmas he made a set of toy soldiers, some wooden mice and dollies, and they were the toys the children played with the most. They couldn't wait to see what he brought them this time.

The grandfather clock downstairs chimed 10 p.m., but Polly was still wide awake. She couldn't stop thinking about her uncle walking through the door in the morning. She poked her brother, but he had fallen fast asleep. So she crept downstairs. Dad was sat by the fire, cracking nuts with his favourite nutcracker. Uncle Sid had made it for Dad last year.

A stair creaked and Dad looked up. Polly looked at Dad. Dad looked at Polly. Dad sighed. "Come on down, young lady," he said.

Polly snuggled up by the fire. Dad passed her the nutcracker while he went to the kitchen to get some chocolate biscuits and a hot drink to dunk them in.

"Keep on cracking while I'm gone," Dad said. "We've got a nut roast to make tomorrow!"

While Dad was gone, Polly cracked almonds and hazelnuts and pecans. The bowl was filling up with all the sweet nut kernels and she was having lots of fun, but then she reached for a huge walnut. CRUNCH! The nutcracker split in two. Polly's eyes widened in horror. The poor nutcracker. What was Dad going to say?

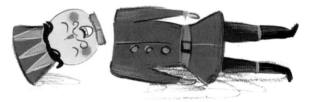

BONNNNNNNG! Out of the blue, the grandfather clock chimed. Polly jumped a mile in the air and dropped the nutcracker on the floor. CREEEEEAAAAKKKKK. The lid of her toy box opened, all on its own. Polly squeezed her eyes tight and opened them again. There, clambering out of the toy box and marching across the floor was a army of toy soldiers, led by the mice, with the peg dollies bringing up the rear. They were heading towards the nutcracker.

The toy army formed a circle around the nutcracker and drew their little weapons.

"No!" Polly cried.

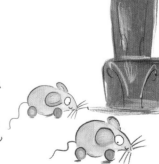

Then the mice pulled the ribbons from the dolls's hair and laid them across the nutcracker's broken body. The soldiers stood guard as the dolls wrapped their ribbons around the nutcracker. Each of them gave him a little kiss, then they turned and marched back to the toybox, climbing back inside and closing the lid behind them.

BONNNNNNNG! The grandfather clock chimed again.

"Two cups of tea and a plate of chocolate dippy cookies," Dad announced, coming back into the room.

Polly burst into tears.

"I'm so sorry, Dad! I broke the nutcracker. I'm so so so sorry."

"Why are you crying, Polly?" Dad said.

He picked up the nutcracker from the floor. It was whole again.

Polly's tears dried at once. It was magic. She took the nutcracker and gave him a kiss of her own, then she snuggled up with Dad, dunking their biscuits in their tea and cracking nuts until Polly's eyes became heavy.

As Dad carried Polly up to bed, she peered over his shoulder. The toy box lid lifted just a crack and three little heads poked out. Polly smiled sleepily and closed her eyes. She knew she was going to have magical dreams, and when she woke up, Uncle Sid would be there.

Polly finally fell fast asleep.

DIPPY CHOCOLATE BISCUITS

These biscuits are all about the dipping. Not only are they dipped in chocolate, they are just made for dunking into a lovely warm cuppa on a winter's day. Why not try them with the chai latte from page 140?

Makes 20

Ingredients

125g unsalted butter, softened

100g dark muscovado sugar

1 tbsp treacle

1 large egg yolk

225g plain flour, sifted

½ tsp bicarbonate of soda

150g milk chocolate

50g unsalted butter

Method

Preheat the oven to 160°C fan/gas mark 4. Line two baking trays with baking paper.

Cream the butter and sugar in a medium bowl until light and fluffy.

Add the treacle and egg yolk and mix well.

Add the flour and bicarbonate of soda and mix until it all comes together as a dough.

Take a large teaspoonful of the dough and roll into a ball. Place it on one of the trays and flatten slightly with a fork. Make sure each ball of dough is about 2.5cm apart.

Bake for 15–18 minutes.

Remove from the oven and transfer to a wire rack to cool completely.

Meanwhile, make the chocolate dip by melting the chocolate and the butter in a microwave or in a small ovenproof bowl set over a pan of simmering water.

Lay out some fresh baking paper. Dip half of each biscuit in the melted chocolate and leave to set on the baking paper.

NUT ROAST

This is a simple alternative to a traditional roast dinner. You could even have it for your Christmas dinner, topped with the Roasted Tomato Sauce! (Recipe on the next page.) Everyone will have something they can have a go at in the method, from the youngest to the eldest in the family.

Serves 8-10

Ingredients

20g unsalted butter

3 garlic cloves, peeled and crushed

1 small onion, chopped

2 tbsp tomato purée

200g button mushrooms, chopped

1 yellow pepper, chopped

1 large carrot, peeled and grated

1 tsp salt

1 tsp paprika

150g red split lentils

400ml vegetable stock

100g fine breadcrumbs (dried or fresh)

150g mixed unsalted nuts, coarsely chopped

3 large eggs, lightly beaten

100g mature Cheddar cheese, grated

handful of finely chopped coriander, about 3 tbsp

Method

Preheat the oven to 160°C fan/gas mark 4. Grease the inside of a 900g loaf tin and line the base with baking paper.

Put the butter, garlic, onion, tomato purée, mushroom, pepper, carrot and salt in a large pan. Cook on a medium heat for 5 minutes, until everything has softened.

Add the paprika, lentils and vegetable stock and cook for 10 minutes or until all the moisture has evaporated.

Take the mixture off the heat and transfer to a large bowl. Leave to cool for 15 minutes.

Mix in the breadcrumbs, nuts, eggs, cheese and coriander. Make sure everything is incorporated, then spoon it into the tin, packing it all in nice and tight.

Bake in the oven for 50 minutes to 1 hour. It should be firm on top when cooked.

Remove from the oven and leave to cool in the tin for 10 minutes before turning out.

129

ROASTED TOMATO SAUCE

You only need one roasting dish to make this easy, delicious sauce. It is sweet and tangy and works beautifully with the Nut Roast.

Serves 8-10

Ingredients

800g ripe tomatoes, quartered

50ml olive oil

½ tsp salt

1 tsp brown sugar

3 garlic cloves, peeled and chopped

2 tbsp balsamic vinegar

large handful of parsley, roughly chopped

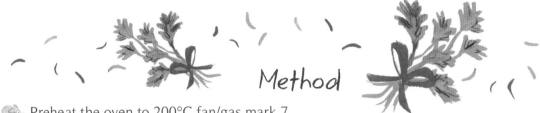

Method

- Preheat the oven to 200°C fan/gas mark 7.

- Put the tomatoes, oil, salt, sugar, garlic and balsamic vinegar into a large roasting pan.

- Give everything a good stir and bake in the oven for 30 minutes.

- Remove from the oven, give everything another good stir and place it back in the oven for a further 30 minutes.

- Remove from the oven and leave to cool for 10 minutes.

- Carefully spoon the mixture into a blender. Add the parsley and blitz to a smooth paste. You can add a little trickle of water if necessary to loosen the sauce.

- Serve while still warm. If serving later, gently warm it up in a small pan first.

NADIYA'S TIP
This also makes a fantastic pasta sauce. Just stir it through
freshly cooked pasta for a tomatoey treat of a tea.

'Twas the Night of
MUM'S PARTY

'Twas the night of Mum's party, when all through the house,
Everything was rockin' – even the mouse.
Decorations were hung by the banisters with care,
With fairy lights glittering everywhere.

The children were jumping up and down on their beds,
While visions of party food danced in their heads.
Grandma was busy with a sudoku or three,
And Auntie was making a chowder for tea.

When outside the window, the kids heard a sound,
They bounced off their beds to see who was around.
The moon shone brightly on the glistening snow,
And lit up a figure in the garden below.

A man dressed in fur, and then – what should appear?
A sleigh full of goodies and eight flying reindeer!
He whistled, and shouted, and called them by name,
As across the tall treetops the animals came.

"Come Dasher! Come, Dancer! Come, Prancer and Vixen!
Here, Comet! Here, Cupid! Here, Donner and Blitzen!"
The kids gaped at each other with shock on their face
As the reindeer landed with elegant grace.

The misty air blew and they pranced in the street.
All stood in a line, so proud on their feet,
The whole team were in an excitable mood
With their sleigh piled with presents and party-time food.

Listen! Are those footsteps at the top of the drive?
Could it be? Is it him? Is he about to arrive?
Bang bang bang! A knock at the door.
The kids tumbled downstairs, and guess who they saw?

His eyes – how they twinkled! His dimples, how merry!
His cheeks were like roses, his nose like a cherry!
With a chuckle, a grin and a nod of his head,
He let the kids know they had nothing to dread.

"Are you here for the party?" they heard Auntie ask.
But he didn't reply – he went straight to his task.
Then Grandma gave him cake and chai latte to drink
as he brought in some presents with a smile and a wink

After he'd finished, he sprang to his sleigh,
And the eight prancing reindeer took off straightaway.
But the kids heard him shout, as he flew out of sight,
"Happy Birthday to Mum, and to all, a good night!"

136

SWEETCORN CHOWDER

It's my birthday on Christmas Day, and sweetcorn chowder is often on the menu at my party. It is a rich dish with a thick creamy sauce that is all made in one pan. It's so quick and easy to make, it leaves lots more time for party games!

Serves 4

Ingredients

50g unsalted butter

1 garlic clove, peeled and crushed

1 small onion, finely chopped

2 small potatoes, peeled and diced into 1cm chunks

230g sweetcorn, canned or frozen

½ tsp smoked sweet paprika

3 tsp plain flour

500ml skimmed milk

5g chives, finely chopped

salt and black pepper

Method

* Put the butter in a medium pan over a medium heat.

* Wait for the butter to melt, then add the garlic and onions, and season.

* Cook the onions for 5 minutes, until starting to colour and soften.

* Add the diced potatoes and cook for 6–8 minutes, until they are slightly translucent around the edge. If your potato chunks are on the big side, this may take a little longer.

* Add the sweetcorn and the paprika and cook for 2–3 minutes. If you are using frozen sweetcorn, this may take a little longer – just be sure the kernels have cooked through properly.

* Add the flour to the mixture and cook for 2 minutes, stirring all the time.

* Pour in the milk and leave to simmer for 10–12 minutes, until the chowder has thickened.

* Take off the heat and stir in the chopped chives.

COCONUT CREAM CHAI LATTE

This is a kids' version of the creamy chai latte that grown-ups have in a coffee shop. You only need a little bit of the spice mix each time, so store the rest in a container for the next time you want to make the drink. Cheers!

Serves 2

Ingredients

400ml tin of coconut milk, chilled in the fridge for 1 hour or more

1 tsp vanilla bean paste or vanilla extract

4 tbsp ground cardamom powder

1 tsp ground cloves

2 tbsp ground cinnamon

1 decaffeinated teabag

1 tbsp honey

Method

✳ Open the tin of coconut milk. There should be a solid layer of cream on top. Scoop it out and place in a bowl. Add the vanilla and whip for a few minutes until light and fluffy.

✳ Put all the spices in a small bowl and mix well.

✳ Put the teabag and remaining coconut milk from the tin into a saucepan, then place on a low heat to warm the milk.

✳ Add half a teaspoon of the spice mixture to the milk and give everything a stir. Bring the mixture to the boil, then turn the heat down to low.

✳ Add the honey and stir again. Heat gently for 2 minutes more.

✳ Remove the teabag, making sure to squeeze it out into the pan first.

✳ Pour the chai into two mugs and dollop the whipped coconut cream on top.

✳ Allow to cool down a little, then sprinkle a tiny pinch more of the spice mixture on top and serve.

MINCEMEAT CAKE

Who doesn't love a mince pie? I certainly do! That delicious, sweet, sticky filling is soooo good. Here, I'm taking that sticky goodness I love so much and making it into a cake instead of a pie.

Serves 8-10

Ingredients

140g unsalted butter, softened

140g light brown sugar

2 medium eggs

225g self-raising flour, sifted

410g jar of mincemeat

85g candied lemon peel

25 whole almonds

3 tbsp honey or golden syrup

Method

✳ Preheat the oven to 170°C fan/gas mark 5. Grease a 20cm round springform cake tin and line with baking paper.

✳ Cream the butter and sugar until pale and fluffy.

✳ Add the eggs one at a time, mixing well after each one.

✳ Fold the sifted flour into the mixture.

✳ Add the mincemeat and lemon peel and give it all a good stir.

✳ Pour the cake mixture into the tin and level it off.

✳ Add the whole almonds on top in whatever pattern you fancy!

✳ Bake in the oven for 1 hour 15 minutes. Check halfway through baking, and if you find that the cake is browning too much on top, cover it with a sheet of foil.

✳ Check the cake is baked by inserting a skewer into the middle. If the skewer comes out clean, the cake's ready.

✳ Remove from the oven and leave to cool for 15 minutes in the tin.

✳ Take the cake out of the tin and leave it to cool completely on a wire rack.

✳ Once cool, brush the cake with the honey or golden syrup.

143

Thank you

To my children Musa, Dawud and Maryam, who relentlessly taste-test all my recipes, even after they have been cooked a dozen times. Sometimes you are a bit too honest, but thank you for being so encouraging about the stories and the recipes. You guys are my live-in guinea pigs and when you willingly unload the dishwasher I know I must be doing something right.

Thanks to the team at Hodder Children's Books and Hachette Children's Group: Emma, Alison, Anne, Fritha, Becky, Lucy, Katy and Hilary. My simple idea wouldn't even have made it off the ground without your support, and I am so proud of how it has evolved. Let's hope this book soars to great heights too.

Thank you to photographers Adam Lawrence and Georgia Glynn Smith, and food stylists Lisa Harrison, Anna Burges-Lumsden and Sophie Mackinnon. And to Clair Rossiter, so many thank-yous. The photos and illustrations truly bring living, breathing air to this book.

To all the people who have supported this book and the first Bake Me a Story, the biggest thank you goes to you for taking time to read and create with your little ones. There is no point in writing without people to read. So for as long as you will read, I will write.

This festive season, let us celebrate all that is good in the world. Let us share, be kind and have fun and laughter in our homes – especially in our kitchens. Hold tight to the people you love and create memories that will last forever.

That is exactly what I intend on doing.

SHORTLISTED FOR THE
BRITISH BOOK AWARDS 2017

NADIYA'S

Bake Me a Story

OUT NOW!

15 original
STORIES and
15 brand-new
RECIPES

'A wonderful gift for all aspiring bakers.'
Evening Standard

'Brings families into the kitchen to spend
time sharing stories and cooking.'
Gransnet.com

'A host of easy-to-follow recipes
for young chefs.'
Scottish Daily Express

#BakeMeaStory

HODDER